Library of Congress
Control Number: 2024920806

Dedication

I dedicate this book to my son Michael Jr. Stanley, who visited Guyana and was able to attend the bi-centennial anniversary of the Demerara Slave Rebellion of 1823. This book is also dedicated to all the children of my ancestors, and to my husband Mr. Michael Stanley, who encourages me to write the stories which are so much a part of our ancestors.

My ancestors gathered around a fire in a little village on the east coast of Demerara in Guyana. They clapped their hands and cried out to the great and unseen king of heaven, and of all the earth.

"Take us back home. We don't want to be slaves. We miss the yams and corns of Africa. Yes, we miss the sweet fruits of the soil of Africa. We miss the taste of the prickly okras, which smiled at the rising of the sun."

The great and unseen king
spoke through the clouds.

"I see your tears you Ashanti,
Yoruba, Ibo, Mandingo, Bakongo
and all tribes here from Africa.
This is your new home."

"What was that sound I heard
from high above?"

"O king, that was our clapping,"
said my ancestors.

"What Do You Clap?"

"What Do You Clap?"

"What Do You Clap?"

The king's voice was louder and lauder each time he spoke

My ancestors became afraid,
then one of the elders of the
Yoruba tribe said in a trembling
voice,
"We....... We clap our hands
as we call
as we call to you,
O Great King.
O Great King."

"Now tell me, look all around you."

"What Do You See?"

"What Do You See?"

"What Do You See?"

Said the voice of the great
and unseen king.

My ancestors began to look
with keen eyes.
"We see the coconut palm trees."

"Now, Go and make good use of it."

"She is the Mother of all Trees."

"You shall not only clap your palms to call me, but clap with praises unto to me. Go, and make good use of the coconut tree!"

My ancestors began to make many things from the coconut palm tree.

They picked the young coconuts and drank the water of the coconut tree.

They ate the juicy hearts which gave them strength of the coconut tree.

They enjoyed the jiggly jelly
of the coconut tree.

They grated the coconut, and drank the juice of the coconut tree.

They cooked Metemgee and cook-up rice with the milk of the coconut tree.

They baked bread, cakes, buns and all kinds of sweet treats from the couscous of the coconut tree.

They made ropes, soaps, hair and skin products from the magnificent parts of the coconut tree.

They made and cooked foods from the rich nutritious oil of the coconut tree.

They carved ornaments, jewelry and buttons from the shells of the coconut tree.

They weaved hats and mats, and made bats, bags and brooms all from the branches of the coconut tree.

They built huts and houses from the trunks of the coconut tree.

They washed their clothes and scrubbed their floors all from the husk of the coconut tree.

They made their beds and rested their weary heads on the fibers of the coconut tree.

They lit fires and cooked their meals all from the parts of the coconut tree.

When the time came and they were free, they clapped their palms and sang with praises as they gazed at the symbol of the coconut tree.

METEMGEE

FAMOUS GUYANESE DISH
MADE WITH COCONUT MILK
AND VEGETABLES

COOK-UP RICE

GUYANESE DISH MADE FROM RICE,
PEAS, VEGETABLES, MEAT AND COCONUT MILK

COUSCOUS

FINE PIECES OF GRATED COCONUT

COCONUT HUSK

FIBER OR PROTECTIVE LAYER OF THE COCONUT

ANCESTORS

A RELATIVE WHO LIVED A LONG TIME AGO

TRIBE

PERSONS OF THE SAME GROUP OR BELIEF

Marlita Stanley

As a child, growing up in Guyana was lots of fun for me. I enjoyed sitting outside in the moonlight, telling stories and listening to my siblings, peers and sometimes the adults sharing the stories, which were passed down to them from our ancestors. Story telling was an important part of my life. I often found myself hurrying home from school, so that I could be at home by 3:45 p.m. to listen to a radio storytelling program by the name of Sunshine Corner. Those early years helped to build my curiosity in reading , writing and story–telling.

As I got older, I became a teacher and taught at Buxton Community High School, on the East Coast of Demerara, Guyana. Later I migrated to the United States of America. I continued to work as an educator in both private schools and with the New York City Department of Education. I love teaching and working with my young students.

A Tree For My Ancestors

1) What is your favorite part of the story?

_____

_____

_____

_____

2) The slaves said, "Take us back home." Where do you think was their original home?

_____

_____

_____

_____

A Tree For My Ancestors

3) Have you ever eaten any foods made from
   coconut? If so, what can you tell about that food.

_____

_____

_____

4) Do you recognize this continent?
   Which continent is it?

_____

_____

_____

A Tree For My Ancestors

Questions related to the story

5) Look at the map, find the country of Guyana.